The Dawn of
the Age
of Aquarius

June Rye

London | New York

Contents

About the Author

June Rye was born and grew up in South Africa and emigrated with her family to England in 1978. Her first book entitled *Be Healthy & Fit the Wholefood Way* was published in South Africa in 1977. Her husband, Charles, sadly passed away in 2013. She has two children and two grandchildren.

Acknowledgements

I wish to thank the following for allowing me to quote certain excerpts from their websites:
The Origin of Religion published by AllAboutGOD.com Ministries, M. Houdmann; P. Matthews-Rose; R. Niles, editors, 2002-2012.
Astrological Ages. Wikipedia free encyclopaedia.
Lost City of Petra. National Geographic.

I'd like to thank Colin Timms for the original cover design.
Website: www.theelectronicbookcompany.com
Contact: colin.timms@theelectronicbookcompany.com

I'd also like to acknowledge Alice Kennedy, talented graphic designer, for her assistance with the cover design.
Website: http://alicekennedy.wixsite.com/aykdesign
Contact Page: http://alicekennedy.wixsite.com/aykdesign/contact

And last but not least, my thanks to my editor Kimberley Humphries for the help and interest she showed in reorganising the chapters in this revised copy of *The Dawn of the Age of Aquarius*.
Website: http://www.morethan-words.com
Contact: kimberley@morethan-words.com / 07754 778910

Introduction

Have you ever lost a loved one or been seriously injured in an accident? You may have felt as if you were trapped in a deep black pit of despair, asking questions like 'Why me?' or 'Why do bad things always happen to me?". If you have, then this book may help you to understand the reasons why, as I have felt that despair too, but also found many answers from a most unexpected source. I would very much like to share these with you, and it is my sincere hope that my findings might help you with your pain.

Many years ago, I was a practising nutrition consultant, using radiesthesia (dowsing) as a diagnostic tool, and decided to investigate where this psychic phenomenon was coming from. I didn't believe in a particular god, but I did feel that there was some force, or energy, within me to enable me to ascertain which foodstuffs were causing a client's particular ailment. This was the start of my quest for enlightenment.

But this is the story of how that quest turned into one of the most turbulent periods of my life, which began in 1985 and only stopped in 2009. For many years, my mind was bombarded with my past life memories, as well as visions going back as far as 10,000 BC. I have written this book to explain a little about such matters as religion and reincarnation, the phenomena of the pyramids and other ancient constructions, and to throw a little light on what life on Earth is all about, among other things that mystify us.

And although I have written this book from a Christian point of view as opposed to an eastern point of view, the same philosophy applies to all the souls, whatever their faith. The reason for this is that those with a Christian faith are often curious about such things as reincarnation, but may be sceptical or even fearful of examining these concepts for risk of upsetting their Christian families. But it is my belief that the faith a person has is the 'truth' for that individual, and should be respected, and that we should examine and seek to understand each other's faiths without preconceptions or fear.

But to set the scene I am going to tell you first about the astrological ages, and specifically about the Age of Aquarius and why it is so significant to us.

Astrology

Astrology is the study of the movements and relative positions of celestial objects as a means for divining information about human affairs and terrestrial events. Astrology has been dated to at least the second millennium BCE (Before our Common Era), and has its roots in calendrical systems used to predict seasonal shifts and to interpret celestial cycles as signs of divine communications. Many cultures have attached importance to astronomical events, and some – such as the Indians, Chinese and the Mayans – developed elaborate systems for predicting terrestrial events from celestial observations. Western astrology, one of the oldest astrological systems still in use, can trace its roots to the nineteenth through to the seventeenth centuries BCE in Mesopotamia, from where it spread to Ancient Greece, Rome, the Arab world and eventually central and western Europe. (This is not to be confused with astronomy, the scientific study of celestial objects.)

Astrological Ages

An astrological age is a time period in astrology which is believed by some to parallel major changes in Earth's inhabitants' development, particularly relating to culture, society and politics. There are twelve astrological ages corresponding to the twelve zodiacal signs in astrology. At the completion of one cycle of twelve astrological ages, the cycle repeats itself. Astrological ages occur because of a phenomenon known as the 'precession of the equinoxes'. One complete period of this precession is called a 'great year' or 'platonic year' of about 25,920 years.

An astrological age varies because it is specified by the amount of time taken for the vernal equinox point to move all the way through a particular constellation of fixed stars, and the constellations come in a variety of sizes; hence, the astrological age associated with a large constellation – Virgo, for example – is much longer than that of a small constellation such as Scorpio.

An astrological age for a constellation begins with the vernal equinox point moving into that constellation, as seen from Earth. It ends when the vernal equinox point moves out of that constellation again, as seen from Earth. We are now at the very beginning of the Age of Aquarius which will last for the next two thousand years. There are two broad approaches about the effects upon the world due to the astrological ages. Some believe the changes on Earth are caused and marked by the influences of the given astrological sign associated with the age, while others do not follow the causative model and believe it is a matter of synchronicity. Despite all references provided by various sources, astrologers cannot agree upon the exact dates of the beginning and ending of the ages.

Many astrologers find the ages too erratic based on either the vernal point moving through the randomly sized zodiacal constellations or sidereal zodiac, and instead round all astrological ages to exactly 2000 years each. In this approach, the ages are usually neatly aligned so that the Taurus age is found from 4000 BC to 2000 BC, the Aries age from 2000 BC to 1 AD, the Pisces age 1 AD to 2000 AD, and the Aquarian age 2000 AD-4000 AD and so on. This approach is not consistent with the precession of the equinoxes, however, as based on precession of the equinoxes, there is a one-degree shift approximately every seventy-two years; therefore, a thirty-degree movement requires 2160 years to complete.

Historical Similarities
of the Ages

Taking it as 2000 years per age, starting with Taurus, the following provides a very brief resume of the ages:

The Age of Taurus - The Bull: 4000 BC to 2000 BC. Bull-worshiping cults began to form in Assyria, Egypt and Crete and relate to Taurus symbolizing the bull. Copper and bronze was smelted for the first time and worked into bronze swords during the early phase of this era. Papyrus was invented and pyramids were built around 3000 BC.

The Age of Aries - The Ram: 2000 BC to 1 AD. Nations such as China, Persia, Greece and Rome started expanding their empires. Iron ore was smelted for the first time and worked into iron swords, and the development of social aspects, sciences and arts started in Ancient Greece. This age also ushered in efforts to replace polytheism with monotheism. Moses, the biblical Hebrew religious leader and prophet, condemns his own people upon finding them worshipping a golden calf (a symbol of the previous Age of Taurus and of the worship of the bull deity) after coming down from Mount Sinai.

The Age of Pisces - The Fishes: 1 AD to 2000 AD. This age is characterized by the rise of many religions or philosophies such as Christianity, Islam and Buddhism, as well as the industrial and social revolutions and continuous research into the truth hidden behind what is perceived by the five senses.

The Age of Aquarius - The Water Bearer: 2000 AD to 4000 AD. An age of enlightenment and personal freedom, technology, medical research, and individual spiritual awakening en masse, which although not organized, is forming a worldwide humanitarian yet unemotional era of spiritual clarity and spontaneous friendship. According to an esoteric Christian tradition, such as the Rosicrucians, the proximity and entrance into the Age of Aquarius – occurring after the Age of Pisces, or the age ruled by the sword – will bring to those older souls who have now evolved through the Christian Era of the past 2000 years, the real knowledge of the inner and deeper meaning of the Christian teachings. When Nostradamus wrote that the Age of Aquarius is the beginning of an 'anti-Christ period', I interpret that as turning away from the religious dogma of the previous age, while still retaining the spiritual and moral teachings of the Christian faith.

Now that we have a better understanding of the astrological ages, I will explain to how my journey to enlightenment began, why and how my understanding and visions increased, and the effect they had on my life and my family. I must add that I am merely a messenger now able to put these experiences into words, and I hope you will benefit from a better understanding of our lives as humans, and be able to enjoy a greater insight into other dimensions so different to ours, but so connected.

My Quest for Enlightenment Turned into a Nightmare

It all began on the 25th of May 1985 while I was attending a weekend course on chakras (energy force centres in the body) and crystal healing in London.

Some years before, I had taken a course in naturopathy and radiesthesia (dowsing with the aid of a pendulum) and was practising as a nutrition consultant using the pendulum to detect which foodstuffs could be the underlying cause of a particular ailment, and then planning a suitable diet for the client. I was getting very good results with this method, but by 1985 I started wondering where this psychic phenomenon, or whatever it was, was coming from. As I've explained, I didn't believe in a god, but I did wonder how this energy, or force within me, was working, and why I was able to do this.

On that first day in London, we learned about the various chakras and crystal healing, and how the energy force of a certain crystal can heal a particular chakra. Then we had to sit in a circle, close our eyes and imagine sitting in a beautiful place, think of a colour and breathe it in and feel its aura calming us. After a while, however, I found this extremely boring and wished I could go home.

After lunch, we learned a bit more about the healing power of the crystals, and then had to do this sitting and thinking about colours bit again – and again, I admit I wished I could go home. But suddenly I got the shock of my life. In my head appeared a picture of me as a young girl sitting in a church reciting the rosary in French. I knew it was me, because I felt so comfortable in my surroundings, as if I knew the place. It was such a shock that I burst into tears. The teacher came and put her arms around my shoulders and said, 'It's OK, there's nothing to be afraid of. I was told you were coming, because the time has come for you to learn more about your part in and the purpose of your present life.' Understandably I was somewhat upset and didn't want to stay any longer, but she told me it was important to make an appointment to pay her a visit the following week.

To this day, I don't know how I managed to get to Liverpool Street Station and get the train back home. I sat on the train in a daze, wondering how this could have happened to me, a down-to-earth, ordinary person who grew up in an Afrikaans farming community in rural South Africa, the daughter of a cattle farmer and a music teacher.

By the time I got home I had a very bad migraine and went straight to bed; but I lay awake most of the night thinking about what had happened. I knew about reincarnation, but never in a million years thought I would ever experience anything like this. I told my husband the next morning, but he thought it was my imagination and told me to forget about it.

The following week, I went to see the teacher. She told me some personal things about myself, which were true, and then explained that she couldn't help me further as her task was done, and she could 'see' that I was about to go on a long journey of enlightenment, and that I would have to work it out by myself without any outside help. Needless to say, I was somewhat confused, and didn't really know what she meant by all this. Little did I know this 'journey' was going to take twenty difficult years.

Gradually the visions became more frequent, and after a month or so I couldn't cope with my business and gave that up. I was so confused, but obviously still had to look after the housekeeping and the family. My poor husband was at his wits' end trying to get me to see our GP, but I refused point-blank to seek advice from the medical profession. Can you imagine where I might have landed up!

Sometimes the visions would stop for a few weeks but then they would start up again. This went on for many years and, understandably, it was very distressing for the family, but there was no way to stop the pictures in my head. I found the visions would stop after a few units of alcohol, which seemed to anaesthetise my mind, but obviously, I couldn't drink all the time because I had to use the car to do the shopping, and I had to do the housework and prepare the meals. (I know now that 'what will be, will be', and that everything that happens in life has a purpose; but that does not make what happened back then any easier.)

My husband retired in 1993 at the age of seventy. Needless to say, the following years didn't go at all well – but that is a personal and private matter. Suffice to say, life eventually became bearable for the family when the visions stopped.

Up until then, however, I existed in a deep pit of despair, wishing for someone to stretch out a hand and help me out of the black hole. Night after night I would see various pictures, which didn't seem to make sense. And as well as the visions I saw in my mind, I was also being guided to read up on various subjects – but I will explain about that later on in the book. Imagine three or four boxes of different puzzles emptied into a heap and then picking up a piece at a time and trying to find another piece which would fit into it. That is how I felt. Gradually, over the years, I was able to fit the pieces together in order to complete the various puzzles, however, and I will also explain these puzzles too; but first, I would like to tell you about how the images appeared in my mind and then past life visions.

How the Visions Appeared in my Mind

I felt familiar and comfortable with the pictures from my subconscious, as if I already knew about the subject, and the pictures popping into my mind from the outside were sometimes in the form of symbols or cartoons, which were easy to understand. For instance, when I was reading about the Great Pyramid being built circa 2500 BCE, an image of a lion in the sky and the number 10,000 kept flashing into my mind. I realised I was being reminded that the Great Pyramid was constructed around 10,000 BCE during the Age of Leo. That vision was a reminder to me that I was alive on Earth at that time, and I felt very comfortable with this memory. Also, when I saw my past lives, I knew immediately that it was me and I could understand the language that was being spoken. I'll tell you a bit more about these now.

Past Life Visions

At first, I saw glimpses, or 'pieces', of myself in various countries – just a glimpse of one puzzle piece – and then month after month the pieces would gradually build into a picture of a past life, and these past visions came out of my subconscious mind. I felt comfortable in each picture, and knew which country I was in, as I've explained, because of the language that was being spoken and which I could understand. I could also see how my life ended and what date it was. I had four past life visions: from Italy, Spain, Germany and France. My life in France was the one before this one – that was the life I first got a glimpse of when I went on the crystal healing course – and I died of TB at the age of twenty-four. I also saw how the work I had done in those four lives had a bearing on the life I was in now. The only other life I saw was my daughter's immediate past life, the reason being that there is a connection between us through the Carmelite Order.

During the past 2000 years of the Age of Pisces I have only ever reincarnated into the Christian Catholic religious orders. My task then was to help spread the word of the Catholic Church; whereas in this life, my ultimate task is to assist with the transition period between the two ages.

In my very first life in the Christian era, I was born in Italy in 480 AD, and at a very young age was sent to live amongst the Benedictine nuns, an order which was in it's infancy at that time. I died there in 547. Another life was in Germany from 1098-1179, and once again in the Benedictine Order. A third was in 1515-1582 as a Carmelite in Spain, and the last life I was shown I was again in the Carmelite Order 1873-1897, but this time in France. This is the first life I have been born into as a Protestant in a Protestant family.

(I must emphasise that my soul went through many more lives than the four mentioned in the Christian era above, and through hundreds of lives before that period.)

Study Time

This lasted on and off for many years, and these visions were different, as instead of appearing in my mind from my subconscious, these pictures popped into my mind from the outside. I would get a glimpse of a certain subject, which would continue to float in and out of my mind until I got the book from the library. When I had finished the book, another subject would appear, and so on. I did not have access to the internet at that time, so these trips were time-consuming and involved travel. Also understand that while the visions and studying was going on, I was also trying to cope with all the normal daily happenings in life.

The following are some of the subjects I had to read up on: the various religions and beliefs; the lives of a few saints who had experienced visions; Nostradamus; the Rosicrucians; the autobiographies and work of some of the more popular psychics and clairvoyants who appear on television; William Blake; Francis Bacon; theosophy; works by Blavatsky and Besant, incorporating Indian and Tibetan mysticism with Christianity, and Rudolf Steiner's anthroposophy, incorporating the Gospels with European mysticism; astrological ages; Edgar Cayce; crop circles; ley lines; dimensions (spiritual planes); ancient monuments and pyramids; the Nazca lines in Peru; and stone circles and Petra in Jordan. (There were a few times while I was studying a particular subject, that a vision would pop into my mind contradicting the information I was reading about, and this will be discussed later in the relevant chapters.)

I have read many biographies written about psychic and paranormal experiences, but the following six books helped me to stop doubting the visions which came from my subconscious, as well as those which came into my head from the outside:

1. The book *Flight into Freedom and Beyond*, the autobiography of Eileen Caddy (1917-2006) co-founder of the Findhorn Community. This brave lady's life was turned upside down for many years by the messages she received from God dictating every aspect of her and her second husband Peter's lives. This book gave me hope in my darkest hour. Findhorn received the United Nations International Decade Award for building a culture of peace in 2001-2010.

2. Jenny Cockell's book *Yesterday's Children*. For many years, Jenny had dreams of living as Mary, a young Irishwoman, dying alone and desperately worried at the thought of leaving her children behind. With much searching, she found Mary, who had died twenty years before she, Jenny, was born. She finally uncovered the past, finding her lost children and reuniting her family.

3. Dr Ian Stevenson (1918-2007) *Where Reincarnation and Biology Intersect*. Stevenson was a professor of psychiatry at University of Virginia Medical School, and spent many years investigating claims by children, in many countries, who could remember a past life. He checked documents, letters, autopsy records, birth and death certificates, hospital records and the like.

4. *Children's Past Lives – How Past Life Memories Affect Your Child* by Carol Bowman, a past life therapist and

researcher. Her extraordinary investigation was sparked when her young son Chase described his own past life death on a Civil War battlefield, an account so accurate it was authenticated by an expert historian. Even more astonishing, Chase's chronic eczema and phobia of loud noises completely disappeared after he had the memory.

5. Dr Raymond J. Moody, renowned for his research into near-death experience (NDE). Since the publication of *Life after Life*, a multi-million copy bestseller, hundreds and thousands of people contacted Dr Moody with their own true stories, leading to a startling new discovery – the shared death experience. In his latest book, *Glimpses of Eternity*, he explores the phenomenon of shared death experiences.

6. The books written by psychiatrists and psychologists, such as Dr Michael Newton's *Journey of Souls* and *Memories of After Life*, Dr Brian Weiss' *Many Lives, Many Masters* and *Only Love is Real*, and Dr Roger J Woolger's *Other Lives, Other Selves*.

I read many books by other authors, but the aforementioned authors and their books made the most impression on me.

Many years later, in 1998, I came across *Heaven's Mirror* by Graham Hancock and Santha Faiia. As I looked at the beautiful pictures of the Hindu and Buddhist cities of Angkor Wat and Angkor Thom in Cambodia, I had the strangest illusion of having been to those places many centuries before. The same happened in places like Mexico and Peru. But I was very disappointed that I wasn't allowed to 'see' when I had actually been to those places.

Before I started on this quest I will admit I was very sceptical about psychics and clairvoyants, but I've come to understand how comforting it must be for the bereaved to receive a message, no matter how trivial, as proof that their loved ones still exist in another dimension.

Other Visions

There were times, while I was studying a particular subject, that a vision would pop into my mind contradicting the information I was reading about. It gradually became clear to me that this traumatic experience, which went on for so many years, was a message that the new information must be published at a later date. Periodically over the years, when I sometimes wondered when this was to be, the thought, *when the time is right* would pop into my mind. Then, towards the middle of 2011, I had a strong urge to write about my visionary experiences. Suddenly I knew the time was *now* and, with the help of the internet, I was able to refresh my memory and review again all those subjects I had read about.

As mentioned before, the only other past life I saw in detail apart from my own was my daughter's; but there were many occasions when I caught a glimpse of the past life of a complete stranger which made me want to burst out laughing! Once, standing in line at the bank, the person in front of me suddenly appeared dressed as a Roundhead. This vision ended as he was walking out of the bank. Another time, in a restaurant, the woman at the next table was dressed very shabbily, while the little boy sitting next to her was covered in soot. (I presumed he had been a chimney sweep!) And one day in the supermarket,

I saw a man on crutches dressed in a WW2 air force uniform. I knew he had been an American because of the chevron on his uniform. And once, on the bus, the man sitting next to me had a tall black Quaker hat on. You can imagine how difficult it was not to start giggling at these times!

The Creation of the Souls

I was not shown the actual beginning of mankind in evolutionary terms, which is thought to have started around about 40,000 BC (or the biblical version of about 6000 years ago).

But I saw a large map of the world, with the continents as they are now, with each country clearly defined. Hundreds of translucent egg shapes then appeared in groups in the various countries, each egg containing a shimmering flame. Gradually the flame split in two and formed into sets of twins in human form, one male and one female, curled up together in the shape of the Chinese yin and yang symbol. The pairs then broke out of the eggs as young adults with their arms about each other. They stayed together for a while, and were then separated and placed into clusters of various other family groups, never in the same group, taking on the features of their particular race and country. (The races of our world are divided into the following four basic groups: Caucasian, Mongoloid and their sub groups, and Negroid and Australoid.)

We are created in family groups and they are our soulmates, and your other half is your twin soul. You are separated right after you were created and do not meet again until your last lives, or on the eighth plane after many centuries if one of you completes life on the Earth plane before the other one; but it is possible that you may catch a glimpse of your twin soul during your various incarnations. Soulmates are souls who have bonded with certain other souls in previous lives – which could have been a parent, a sibling or a friend. Some souls choose to have only one profession or career, and all those at the top of their profession or craft, in every walk of life, are the older souls who have learned their skills throughout many lives. It is not possible to be at the top in this computerised, scientific and technological world we live in today without the experience gained in previous lives.

These very first groups have evolved through *all* the following eras, and are now being born into this new Age of Aquarius. The creation of new souls has been happening periodically through the ages. This we can see by the increase in the world's population.

The Evolution of the Souls Through the Following Eras

Since the beginning of our creation, our human souls have reincarnated century after century within their own racial and family groups, sometimes being absorbed into other nations due to wars and/or invasions. Generally, the citizens must work not only towards the evolution of their own souls, but also for the ultimate advancement of their specific nation towards enlightenment, meaning the tolerance of all others, their viewpoints and beliefs, as well as the spiritual, economic and democratic advancement of their particular nation. (And judging by the present state of the world, this will go on for many thousands of years!)

As I mentioned at the start, I have written this book from a Christian point of view as opposed to an eastern point of view, but believe that the same philosophy applies to all the souls, whatever their faith. A person's faith is their 'truth', and should be respected.

The Origin of Religion

According to the scholars, the origin of religion can be traced to the ancient east and classified in three basic categories:

POLYTHEISM (the belief in many gods) is thought to have originated with Hinduism in about 2600 BC, while others believe it to be around 6500 BC. They view the gods as being in control of all natural events such as rainfall, harvests and fertility, and in ancient times generally believed in sacrifices to appease their gods. There is also a belief in reincarnation, the eastern version being that if one does not behave one's self one could come back as an animal. (The western view being that a soul continues to evolve through many lives to reach full enlightenment.)

PANTHEISM (the belief that all is God) was the belief of the African and American Indian cultures and the later Egyptian religion under the Pharaohs, and Buddhism. The principle of this belief is that God is everything and everything is God. Therefore, nature is part of God and we must live in harmony with nature. Some New Age movements also adhere to this belief.

MONOTHEISM (the belief in one God), which originated with Abraham in about 2000 BC and is the foundation of the Judeo, Christian and Muslim religions.

Reincarnation and Christianity

Educating the Illiterate Masses

Having statues or icons of deities is a simple way of focussing the minds of the illiterate to concentrate on the god they are worshipping. The Greeks had their gods and goddesses: Zeus, Hera, Aphrodite, Hermes, etc. The Romans adopted these gods and changed their names to Jupiter, Juno, Venus, and Mercury etc. Statues were created in their images and temples were built as places for the people to worship and ask for favours.

The Jews believed in and worshipped only one god: God the Father. After the crucifixion, as interest in the early Christian movement grew, the Jews split into two sections: the orthodox Jews stuck to the teachings of the Old Testament (the Torah), while the others followed the teachings of the apostles who retained the Old Testament, and added the New Testament. This group were called Christians.

By the fourth century, when the Roman Empire had gradually converted to Christianity, churches replaced the temples, and the statues became those of Jesus, Mary, Joseph and the apostles, and holy pictures in stained glass windows helped to explain the various sermons or stories in the Bible to the masses. As Christianity progressed over a few more hundred years, statues of the new saints (patron saints) were gradually introduced. These helped the people to focus their prayers on a particular saint to ask for help with a problem, or to ask God, on their behalf, to help with more important requests. For example, if you were an accountant sitting your exam, you could ask St Mathew for help (although he'd probably tell you, you should have studied a bit harder!); if you were a sailor and encountered very bad weather, you might ask for St Scolastica's help, and she would pass your request on to God; or, if you had engine trouble, you'd ask St Patrick for help. House-hunting? St Joseph was the one for that. Unable to conceive? Go to St Mary as she dealt with woman's problems. And St Anthony would help you find lost objects. And so on.

In 1054 AD, the church split into western and eastern Christendoms:

1. Western Christendom was controlled from Rome and came to be known as the Roman Catholic Church (Latin).

2. Eastern Christendom was controlled from Constantinople and was known as the Greek Orthodox Church (Greek).

In the sixteenth and seventeenth centuries (with the Reformation and Henry VIII's break from Rome), the church split again into the following three denominations:

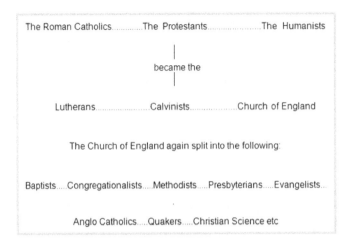

The Roman Catholics............The Protestants...................The Humanists

became the

Lutherans....................Calvinists................Church of England

The Church of England again split into the following:

Baptists....Congregationalists....Methodists....Presbyterians.....Evangelists..

Anglo Catholics.....Quakers.....Christian Science etc

With the Reformation, Protestants no longer thought it necessary to ask a saint to approach God on your behalf. You could now go straight to God or Jesus with your prayers. This went on for a few more years (approximately 100 years), and the older souls had now arrived at the next stage of their evolution. They had learned the Ten Commandments over and over and adopted the values and morals taught by the (Christian) Bible. They had started to leave the dogma of the various Christian religions behind and mature (although not always!) into caring, law-abiding citizens. Many were happy with this situation, but there were others (like myself) who felt that there is, or should be, something more to life, something spiritual – not out there, but something within oneself. It was for that reason I started on my personal journey of discovery.

The Decline of Christianity and the Search for Spirituality

It is estimated that sixty per cent of the world's population believe in reincarnation, and though the vast majority are of eastern origin and do so because it is a central principal of their religion, an increasing number of westerners are beginning to accept this idea. Part of the reason for this steady increase in the belief in reincarnation stems from the growing interest in other spiritual traditions and the acceptance of esoteric teachings, which began when The Beatles and their guru introduced transcendental meditation and eastern ideas to the west in the late 1960s.

During the years between 1980 and 2005, the Church of England, together with the Methodist and Baptist churches, etc., suffered a thirty-one percent decline in their congregation, and the Catholic Church twenty-seven percent. In the 2001 census, seventy-one percent identified themselves as Christians, but only eighteen percent said they were a practicing member of organised religion. There was an increase of thirty-four percent in the Evangelical and Pentecostal churches, and a two percent increase in the Eastern Orthodox Church due to the immigrants from those countries.

More recently there has been an intensification of interest in psychic phenomena and the paranormal as evidenced by the popularity of fictional TV series such as *Medium,* and a string of psychic reality programmes featuring Gordon Smith, Derek Acorah, John Edwards and James van Praagh, etc., whose studio séances have produced evidence of survival after death and brought the subject into the living-rooms of people who would never otherwise have considered consulting a professional psychic.

More and more people are moving away from the dogmatic views of the stricter Christian denominations, joining either the Evangelical or Pentecostal churches; but there are also many turning to psychics, mediums, spiritual healers and past life regressionists in search of the reason for our existence and for proof of an afterlife.

There have been countless incidents of near death or out-of-body experiences. These involve individuals leaving their physical bodies, travelling through a tunnel and emerging in a new world of light and colour to be reunited with loved ones on the other side of physical life. Such incidents are frequently triggered by a physical crisis such as a violent accident, a serious illness, extreme exhaustion or the influence of an anaesthetic. Naturally, they are sent back, however, because their life on the Earth plane is not yet over. A Gallup poll in 1992 suggested that as many as thirteen million Americans believe that they have had an out-of-body experience.

The Three Views of the Soul in our Society

1. That there is an immortal soul that goes from birth to birth until it attains salvation, which ends the rebirth process.

2. That the immortal soul has only one life on Earth and after death is reborn and lives eternally in the spirit world.

3. That there is no immortal soul, but only a kind of energy, which keeps the physical body working until death.

Comment

It's clear to me, one only has to look at the way some parents and their children behave to see they are barely out of the jungle and still have many lessons to learn before they become caring, law-abiding citizens.

And even though I have seen my past lives periodically over several years, it is still not easy to accept that I, as the person I am now in this life, could have been the people I was in my past lives, and that I have become a messenger under instruction to share information in this age.

Before the Reformation, it was the Catholics who went out to convert and educate the masses – building churches, establishing monasteries, convents and schools, first in Europe and then gradually in the second and third worlds. This was absolutely necessary for the advancement of civilisation, and after the Reformation, the other denominations went on to do the same.

I do know the evolutionary stage of the inhabitants of our planet is *exactly where it should be*, but in my opinion, unfortunately, the Catholic Church has stayed trapped in the antiquated views of the Dark Ages, refusing to move forward with the new scientific and social advancement of an ever-changing world (especially in their view regarding birth control). This has caused much of the misery, poverty and overpopulation of many of the poorer nations of the world, and it is my hope that this issue will be sorted out over the next few centuries.

Fastest Growth of Christianity in Africa

According to the Centre for the Study of Global Christianity, the southern hemisphere is taking the lead in growth figures for worshippers. Africa is leading the change with 390 million Christians – more than three times than the number thirty-five years ago.

Despite Roman Catholics and Anglicans being the pioneers of Christianity in African countries, and being the oldest established denominations in the world, the evangelical movement in Africa is very active and has accounted for the overall development of Christianity in the continent.

It is interesting to observe that as the Evangelical Christian movement is spreading in Africa's third world population, the original Christian denominations in the first world (the religions of the west) are gradually losing members. Many of these are the older souls who are gradually awakening out of thousands of years of indoctrination and now have the maturity to understand what is happening to the world around them.

The following pie chart shows the relative support the various religions of the world enjoy:

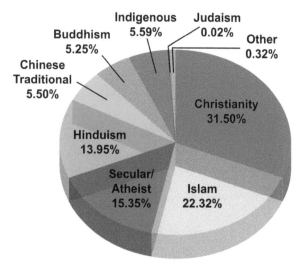

World Religions By Percentage 2012

Dimensions: Spiritual Planes of Existence

I would like to talk about dimensions and planes of existence now, as this is vital for our understanding of other worlds, or states of existence.

Dimensions like radio and TV vary in vibration and frequency, each signal remaining distinct even though they are all jumbled together in the same space. This space where we are at present is filled with countless dimensions (realms) of existence beyond the physical world, all teeming with life, and if we could see and hear those non-physical dimensions, this space would be incomprehensibly crowded and we would be overwhelmed by the sights and sounds of the many entities here amongst us.

I learned about the various dimensions in the following vision: I saw myself standing in the middle of a room filled with thousands of threads in all the colours of the rainbow, pulsating with energy. As I moved out of the room I was able walk right through the threads without breaking their circuits. The coloured threads grouped into straight, wide bands of colours and then reformed into a very large translucent octagonal-shaped pyramid with a flat top – very much like a Mayan pyramid.

There were ten floors, each in a different colour, with the tenth capped in shimmering gold. This vast construction stood just above the ground that was composed of large patches of black, white and grey. People belonging to the various nations and their religious groups were moving in and out of these patches, their emotions changing as they moved through each colour. The ones going through the black patches were experiencing the most agonising emotions such as hate, anger, physical pain, fear, horror and grief. The people in the grey patches seemed neither happy nor sad; while those in the white patches were smiling, laughing, and happily interacting with others on that colour. I realised then that I was being shown that the Earth plane is a place of learning, a place where the soul has to experience every possible aspect of life during many incarnations over a period of thousands of years.

I must emphasise that this is a symbolic picture of heaven with the steps leading up to the ultimate source of creation, and that each colour and number has a specific spiritual meaning with respect to the actual planes are here on Earth where we as humans reside.

The colours were arranged as follows:

First floor – A BRIGHTLY LIT ROOM
Second floor – RED
Third floor – ORANGE
Fourth floor – YELLOW
Fifth floor – GREEN
Sixth floor – BLUE
Seventh floor – DARK BLUE (indigo)
Eighth floor – VIOLET
Ninth floor – PURPLE
Tenth floor – GOLD

First Floor – Brightly Lit and Situated Just Above the Earth
This was a very large space similar to a large airport check-in lounge with desks for each nation. As you can imagine, there

was a continual stream of new arrivals; many were confused, others quietly happy to be 'home'. Souls, on arrival, were always met by a chaperone, which could be their spiritual guide (guardian angel), or sometimes a family member from their personal soul group, or a friend they had known in a previous life. They were escorted to the relevant check-in desk, and once through, moved (or gravitated) to the level they had reached at that particular time on their spiritual path.

Second Floor – Red
Those souls who had died in very painful and shocking circumstances, such as in war situations, and who had endured torture and/or great physical and mental abuse, or had endured a long and painful illness before their death, were met by paramedics and helpers. After going through check-in, they were taken to the second floor (red), to rest in peace for as long it took for them to recover from their ordeal, after which they were assessed before moving to the level they belonged to. I found it very distressing seeing the victims from the countries who believe in the practice of chopping off limbs, and women being burned or stoned to death according to the religious laws of their society because they had been raped or refused to have an arranged marriage.

The second floor also housed all those who had committed crimes against humanity, such as the despots who had murdered and traumatised their own citizens, and those who had committed murder or evil deeds against others. These were mostly young or new souls, who had perhaps only been on the Earth plane for about three or four lives and had not yet learned their lessons.

The circumstances of the families and societies they had been been born into would have shaped their views and ideals, and they were not punished as they would have been on Earth (bearing in mind that many would already have been punished on Earth; i.e. the Nuremberg War Trials, etc.), but they were expected to sit and watch the atrocities they had perpetrated over and over again. The same applied to those who had committed offences such as premeditated murder, child molestation and abuse, cruelty to humans and animals, and so forth. They would already have been punished according to the laws of their society on the Earth plane, and they knew that during some of their future incarnations they would have to experience some sort of evil and abuse at the hands of others. (But if they had killed someone in self-defence, they would not have to experience this again.)

The second floor was where those souls who were so attached to their own anger and grief refused to move on and chose to stay there – which could in some cases be for many centuries. (See the chapter on ghosts and poltergeists.)

The second floor was also where infants and children who'd die young were taken. It is important to mention that new souls on their first few lives *never* die in infancy, they always live through adulthood. On the other hand, *all* babies who die young are older souls, mostly from their own family group, who agree to reincarnate to help the spiritual advancement of their group and also for the purpose of the advancement of medical science.

Examples:

1. A mother whose baby had died of cot death, being an older soul, will have the intelligence to set up a help group for other parents in the same situation, which could spread nationwide. Situations such as this, or any other unexplained deaths, give the reason for more research and scientific advancement for the good of mankind.

2. An infant might die due to a genetic disease. This also then stimulates research into that problem.

Other examples are people who die from degenerative, or other incurable or viral diseases, as these provide another reason for medical and further scientific research. It is also a test for the loved ones who have to cope with the situation, and the patient who agrees to endure these situations. Family members who cope with this situation with love, compassion and understanding are acknowledged and their loving manner noted. In some cases, those who elect to be a patient in similar situations could be paying off a karmic debt.

Floor Numbers Three – Orange; Four – Yellow; Five – Green; Six – Blue; Seven – Indigo

Within all the above planes (three to seven) of existence, are a multitude of concepts, each of which co-exist, like the different rooms in a house. All differ to accommodate the many and varied beliefs. All are equal within their own plane of existence. Each has its own purpose.

Language is not used, as the various groups communicate by telepathy. If you fancy a visit to a particular place, such as a walk in a beautiful park, a swim in the sea, or you wish to explore any place on Earth, you can imagine yourself there. Not physically on the Earth plane, but in your imagination. (I had a vision of a park filled with masses of flowers of every description. This picture gradually moved into various seasons far more beautiful than I had ever seen here on Earth.)

There are great halls of learning, schools, colleges, universities, lecture halls, laboratories and libraries covering technology, economics and all the sciences, as well as academies for all the Arts – music, dance, painting, etc. There are also sports facilities of every description. These subjects are arranged according to the level the souls are on at that particular time. There are buildings constructed that represent the traditions of all the great cultures of the world – cathedrals, temples, mosques, synagogues, and so forth.

The libraries, research labs and all other subjects are set out in a way the souls will understand, at the level intelligence that they are at, at that time, and every member of all the nations study in their own language (or thoughts) and follow their own religious beliefs, or explore any of the other beliefs and languages if they so wish. Unfortunately, the suppressed people in the cultures that are male-dominated will only be at primary or perhaps secondary school level, and the males are the only ones able to study at the higher levels. There is nothing wrong with this situation; they are just following the religious and cultural teachings of their race.

The leaders and prophets of the non-Christian races live at this level, and it is their task to assess the behaviour of their followers on Earth. It must be emphasised that the Koran (Qur'an) does not advocate the killing of infidels, and therefore each individual's behaviour will be assessed on how they have interpreted the message in their holy book.

As we are moving into this new era of enlightenment, the *older* souls of these races are beginning to acquire the knowledge and the courage which enables them to fight for their civil and democratic rights, hence the civil unrest occurring in the Middle East at present.

It must also be remembered that not everyone is at the same stage of his or her evolutionary path, so the simplest way to think of this is in terms of schooling on Earth:

Third – ORANGE as primary school
Fourth – YELLOW as secondary school
Fifth – GREEN as GCSE levels
Sixth – BLUE as A levels
Seventh – INDIGO as university

The souls on the third and fourth levels are still very family orientated and are permitted to contact family members through a medium in order to give them some comfort and proof about their wellbeing. Another reason for this is to gradually get the message across to the masses that there is life after death.

On the fifth and sixth levels, the apron strings are gradually being cut, for although the special bond between the family members will always be there, these souls are maturing and becoming more independent. In future lives they will probably only meet one or two of their soulmates in a particular life. Many of these will also act as helpers during their stay before their next incarnation, when large numbers of people die in catastrophes such as earthquakes, tsunamis, war situations and the like.

Fortunately, it is not all work and no play! On all the levels, there are facilities for sports and/or hobbies the people were interested in while on Earth. Sportsmen and women of the world can practice whatever sport they excel in; the more skilled will eventually become Olympians on Earth.

Those souls who show promise in a certain subject or subjects are encouraged to study at a higher level. They usually tend to follow the same career or profession throughout all their lives and eventually become the leaders and teachers of the various professions and careers in their future lives.

Obviously, there are many teachers in all these large halls of learning, and those from the higher levels teach or guide those of the lower levels. Some are still evolving and do go back to Earth from time to time because they have to experience other lessons, like earning a living, learning to interact with other humans, and experiencing marriage and parenting.

The Seventh Floor – Indigo

This is the gods' university, the nerve centre for the inventions, research and ideas into every aspect of live on Earth to benefit the human race for the following centuries. The tutors are the messengers of the gods (all those who have introduced new concepts, inventions, styles or trends in the past centuries, such as Leonardo da Vinci, Galileo, Albert Einstein, Thomas Edison and many more). I caught a mere glimpse of projects with lasers and computers, and what I assumed to be the assembling of bionic human organs. The pupils will be the future messengers of the gods.

Another part of the university was where the various sections of all the Arts and numerous crafts were being taught.

Strolling past the music section, in my mind I could hear the sounds of every conceivable instrument and style of music being played: tribal, classical piano, orchestral, spiritual, jazz, country and many more. In my mind, I was told the tutors were the messengers of the gods, those who first invented the instruments or composed the various styles of music.

In the dance and movement section, I caught a quick glimpse of Margot Fonteyn and Rudolph Nureyev, and saw them unite into a single flame while they danced and realised they were twin souls. In the modern dance section, I saw Martha Graham, and in another section Fred Astaire. I was shown these souls because before I got married I had been a dance teacher. I felt very privileged that I was able to see them. There were many other sections with souls performing, but I didn't recognise any of them.

It was then that I suddenly realised the meaning of: "In my Father's house are many mansions".

The Hall of Records
This was a large hall containing what looked to me like flat, touch-type computer screens. These could be used to view any part of the history of the world. I saw with a touch on the screen what Earth's crust looked like 200 million years ago, and then with another touch on the screen the continents quickly moved to the positions they are in now. I saw Hannibal crossing the Alps with the elephants. I caught a glimpse of the crucifixion of Jesus and the early Christians being martyred by lions and gladiators in the Colosseum. These visions were very upsetting and I felt physically ill for the next few days. I came to understand that the records of every human being can be traced back to the beginning of their creation, more than 200,000 years ago from the time of the Neanderthal man and woman.

There were many other halls of learning but they weren't shown to me at this time.

The Eighth Floor – Violet

The eighth floor is home to all the twin souls who have reached the end of their particular journey after many incarnations. They are the wise souls who act as guides and helpers behind the scenes to the people on Earth. This is the home of great philosophers and the spiritual leaders and the patron saints of the various religious faiths; it is also where the angels live. These are normal spirits who appear in the guise of an angel to the very religious at a time of great need, because this is the way a 'helper' or 'messenger' from God would be perceived. Some appear in their angelic form, or as they were in one of their former incarnations as American Indians or Tibetan monks, or as guides to mediums or psychics and spiritual healers. There are those who appear in human form to give a helping hand in certain conditions. There are many accounts of someone appearing 'out of the blue' to give assistance to someone in a dangerous or traumatic situation.

The Ninth Floor – Purple

I did not see the inhabitants of this floor. But what I understood from the visions I was shown, was that it is the home of the members of the ancient civilisations who were responsible for building the prehistoric monuments. There were eighty-eight (forty-four males with their forty-four female twin souls), each representing one of the constellations.

The Tenth Floor – Gold

I saw a beautiful vision of a golden penthouse sitting on the top of the multi-coloured pyramid, with the moon and the planets swirling around it. After doing this for a few seconds, they flew into the building one by one. I was being shown that the tenth floor is the home of the gods, and with my mind's eye I saw six tall, blond, handsome couples dressed in flowing, shimmering robes in soft hues of purple, blue and gold. Then, to my amazement, right before my eyes, the robes they were wearing changed into ordinary everyday smart-casual clothes and the words 'God created mankind in his own image' sprang to mind, and I understood that these six men and six women were the supreme beings, the hierarchy, the executive directors of the various aspects of life on Earth. They were the overseers of the evolution of our planet Earth and, together with those beings living on the ninth floor, have been living here on Earth in another dimension for tens of thousands of years. They are the ancients who built the ancient monuments on our planet. (Those who understand the theory of quantum physics and dimensions will know that the vision I saw is quite possible.)

This beautiful vision must have lasted only a few moments, but its message was quite clear to me. The Greeks were guided to believe in the twelve supreme gods who lived on Mount Olympus, and the Romans later adopted those same gods (except they changed their names). After this period came the god of the Christians who lived in heaven with Jesus, the saints and the angels. And now, in this new era, the time has come for us to learn that 'heaven' is actually here on Earth. This will be an era of great scientific and technological advancements, as the understanding of how science and spirituality are interlinked will become clear, and there will be a great awakening of individual spirituality and a worldwide interest in humanitarian issues.

I felt emotionally drained for days after the above encounter, and as the days went past it gradually dawned on me that despite the advancements and awakenings, there will never be peace here on Earth. Or if it ever does happen, it will not be for thousands of years, because Earth is where the human race has to experience and learn about every possible facet of living and being alive.

What I Learned from my Journey Through the Dimensions

Throughout my journey through the dimensions it felt as if I was walking down memory lane, and I especially felt at home on the seventh floor (God's university) and the eighth floor where I recognised Jesus, Mohammad, Krishna and Gandhi. (The spirit of the Dalai Lama was not there, however, as his spirit is on Earth.) They were dressed in ordinary modern cloths. I recognised a few of the patron saints and understood some of them were preparing to reincarnate once again, this time to pass on the New Age message of reincarnation and karma.

Messengers Preparing for Their Next Reincarnation

I then moved to the study room for those belonging to the religious/spiritual section, and observed the way they were studying for their next incarnation into human life on Earth. Their task is to change the original religious philosophies from previous centuries.

Imagine a large round table, and in the middle of this table is a many-facetted pyramid, with pictures and writings about spiritual matters in various languages. Sitting around the table are the many messengers whose task is to be able to explain what they are to teach to the people of the era they are about to reincarnate into. Each one is seeing before them a slightly different picture of the same message; a message for them to relay in their own words and personality of their new life to the people in the social/economic/religious environment of the group they are about to reincarnate into. And this is where they will absorb into their 'being' all aspects of that environment, to become the character and personality which will equip them for their task ahead.

In this group are the future psychiatrists, psychologists, physic mediums, and others schooled in quantum and meta physics, authors, publishers, etc. Many of these messengers have been saints in their past lives. Do not be distracted by the term 'saint', as in their lives on Earth they just walked along the path set out before them and achieved the tasks they were supposed to do. Then many years later, the pope (and his cardinals) saw what good work they had done as founders of the various Catholic orders, and/or their writing regarding religious matters, and decided to give them the title 'saint'.

This is very much the same as the British honours list where MBEs and CBEs and knighthoods are awards which are given to high-achieving people from every section of the community, from school crossing officials and charity workers, to leaders of industry.

Other Messengers from the Seventh Dimension

These are the messengers from the technological, scientific, artistic, social and economic sections of this dimension. They come again and again through the centuries to assist the human race to progress and embrace changes to the original philosophies and inventions from previous centuries.

All the messengers from the above two dimensions are very old souls who have had many lives since 4000-3000 BC and are periodically 'slotted' into the lives of evolving family groups in order to assist the advancement of the human race on the Earth plane.

Your Spiritual Name

During your soul's journey through the ages you will have many names. But you have only the one spiritual name, and that is your given name on the day you were first created. You will have been given a Chinese name, Greek, African, Russian, Egyptian, and so on. It is possible that your spiritual name could be revealed to you once you fully understand your role during a particular time in your life plan.

Your Astrological Natal (Birth) Chart

In the time between your different incarnations, you consult your guides and make a plan for your next incarnation into physical form, deciding upon the path you will follow and the lessons you will learn. You then wait until the planets are in precisely the correct position to support your choices before being born. Therefore, the map of the heavens at the moment of your birth contains significant information about the spiritual life purpose and soul lessons you chose for the life you are about to have.

Most astrologers produce a psychological report, but karmic astrology adds another more spiritual dimension to the psychological approach found in traditional astrology. In eastern philosophies, the law of karma refers to the total effect of a person's actions and behaviour during each incarnation, and is regarded as being the determining factor for the next incarnation.

Non-Believers

Here I am referring to the large group of souls who were brought up in the Christian faith for many centuries before the last two world wars. Having witnessed the atrocities perpetrated, not only during the German Holocaust, but many others which have since happened worldwide, they have lost faith in God and the teachings of the church. Those are the ones who make up the non-believers, the atheists, agnostics and humanists of our time. This group will grow larger over the centuries as their children coming through them will adopt the philosophy of their parents. These souls are in a transition period before they start feeling the urge to search for the spiritual meaning of life. This could take a few lives, but in the meantime, this group will behave with compassion and generosity towards all mankind.

Comment

The above dimensions are how I saw (or was shown) the spiritual realms. The following faiths have different views: the Christian Bible writes about seven realms; Confucianism – two realms; Kabala – five realms; Sufism – four realms; Eckankar – eleven realms; Agnostics – it is not known how many; while humanists and atheists believe there is only one life to be experienced and that is here on Earth.

It must be understood that these views are all true for the individuals belonging to the above faiths, and should be respected.

What is Enlightenment?

Enlightenment is an understanding with absolute certainty that the situation you are in and the path you are on is the one intended for you in this life. It is not a state of mind that you can force yourself into. We all live by the eternal law of cause and effect, and this is a personal journey to find your inner self. Throughout the previous centuries, you have over and over either been someone's child or husband or wife, father or mother, sister or brother, carer or servant, slave or master, the tyrant or the abused, a leader or an underdog. Up until now, through all your previous lives, you have been taught and controlled by the religious choice of your forefathers, and the person you are today is a result of the many experiences you have had in the past, and your talents are all the things you have become good at.

For some, enlightenment is a sudden earth-shattering experience similar to that of Saul's (who became the Apostle Paul) on the road to Damascus. Enlightenment is a kind of landmark you reach and, in a flash, you will 'know' in your heart this is exactly who you are and what your purpose in this life is.

For some, it could be a religious experience, such as seeing a vision of Jesus or any other holy person, and you know instinctively that this is your calling and this is the path you are to follow for the rest of your life.

For others, it could be an experience of unspeakable traumas and abuse, such as the life of Christina Noble to reach the final purpose. In her book *Bridge Across My Sorrows*, she tells of her childhood in a Dublin slum, where she experienced the most horrendous life of sexual abuse while living on the streets, and was later driven to near insanity by overwork and a violent husband. She finds in a dream the will to fight back, eventually ending up in Ho Chi Minh City in Vietnam in 1989 caring for orphaned street children. This eventually lead to The Christina Noble Foundation, and social and medical help centres for poor and unprivileged children in Vietnam and Mongolia, which by the late 1990s had helped over 80,000 children and established fund-raising offices in fourteen countries around the world.

For me, it was a very slow process through all those years of learning and seeing visions that didn't make the slightest sense, and caused many years of confusion and unbelievable stress within our family. At first, alcohol helped to stop the pictures appearing in my mind, as after consuming a few bottles of wine (or something stronger) over a few days the visions would stop, and I'd start feeling bright and alert for a few days, or even weeks. Unfortunately, after a while, the alcohol didn't help to stop the visions, but I found that it did anaesthetise my mind and helped me to cope with the daily mundane chores. It was only my knowledge of nutrition that stopped my liver from being destroyed in the process! I hated myself for the grief I was causing my family and the way I looked. As my weight slowly crept up from size 14 to size 22, I felt completely alone, fat, humiliated and useless. (In South Africa, during my late teens and early twenties, I had been a slim ballet, tap and ballroom dance teacher.)

Later in my forties, I wrote a book on nutrition and healthy living. And when we moved to England in 1977, I studied naturopathy and later practised as a nutrition consultant. My husband had a good job in London, and our children were settled in their schools. I was experiencing one of the happiest times of my life. Then, in 1985, that bubble burst as soon as I went in search of enlightenment. Little did I realise this state of affairs would continue for the next twenty-three years!

The visions stopped as soon as I completed the four puzzles of my past lives, and that was when I *knew* what this experience was all about and how it was connected with those four previous lives: it was to write a book about the reincarnation and the evolution of the soul through many centuries from a Christian point of view. I knew on one hand that this was exactly the reason for this particular life, but on the other hand, I knew this would be very upsetting for my devout Christian South African family – especially my ninety-four-year-old mother who had become very distressed when I first mentioned my visions and past lives, and was convinced that this phenomenon was all to do with the Devil. I didn't mention it for some years, and she (I hoped) had assumed that I had managed to turn my back on this evil situation I had got myself embroiled in. I felt very sad at having to upset her again.

About three months ago, I had a beautiful vision of all the previous visions I had seen throughout those harrowing years. It was shown as a continuous video which seemed to last for only a few minutes. I knew this was a reminder of everything I had learned about, and realised it was time to write this book and that it was to be in the form of an e-book.

And while I was typing this manuscript, there was one short moment, just after I'd written the part about the creation of the translucent eggs, when I experienced the most incredible feeling of joy and warm, comforting love. It was as if someone was standing behind me, folding his arms around me and, for that split second, I knew this was my twin spirit being allowed to comfort me for a few moments, and show me what it felt like when the two flames were reunited.

Unusual Flying Objects

I mentioned before during my study time that I had experienced certain visions contradicting some of the information I was reading about. I once saw in my mind an aircraft I hadn't seen before. After searching the internet, I found some similarities between the Harrier Jump Jet and the helicopter. It looked and behaved like the Harrier Jump Jet without wings but moved slower, much like a helicopter. There were clamp-like arms which could be folded and locked away, very much like the wheels on the undercarriage of an aircraft.

It was able to lift and transport large blocks of stone and set them down in specific places. I saw several of these aircraft going backwards and forwards transporting large blocks of stone from places where they were being shaped with what seemed to be lasers. The first time I saw this aircraft at work was while I was reading about the history of the construction of the Great Pyramid, but the date which appeared in my mind was 10,500 BC not 2560 BC. It was only recently I found the following information below on mystic places, (*Time Life Books,* 1990).

The Great Pyramid at Giza

Below is the generally assumed history of the Great Pyramid:

The Great Pyramid at Giza has a strong astronomical association. The four faces of the pyramid are precisely aligned with the four cardinal points of the compass. It is believed that it was built around 2560 BC and, contrary to earlier belief, the workmen were not slaves, as the pyramid was built long before the Jews arrived in Egypt. Some modern scholars think the pyramid was built by a group of 500-1000 craftsmen assisted by 5000-7000 workmen who came to labour on the monument in shifts from all over Egypt. The houses of some of the workers have recently been unearthed.

The Great Pyramid is the oldest structure on the face of planet Earth, and also the best built. It sits in the exact centre of the landmass of Earth at thirty degrees north and thirty-one degrees east, and is also believed to be precisely at the centre of the gravity of Earth. It consists of over two million stones, none of which weigh less than a ton and some of which weigh twenty tons or more. It is put together with mortar joints that are consistently one-fiftieth of an inch, which is an astounding feat of precision work. It covers over thirteen acres of land with each side measuring over five acres, and is solid throughout other than the pathways and chambers that have been discovered so far. The sides are very slightly concave for unknown reasons, making this the only eight-sided pyramid in existence. This feature can only be seen from the air and only if the light is right. The pyramid has an estimated weight of about 6.3 million tons (one billionth the weight of the Earth itself), and like twentieth century bridge designs, the cornerstones have balls and sockets built into them making it somewhat flexible and enabling it to survive earthquakes and heat expansion.

Did Aliens Build the Pyramids?

The following is an extract from Mystic Places, *Time Life Book*, 1990:

'*More interesting facts related to the measurements of the pyramid are listed below:*

- *There are 36,525 pyramid inches in the perimeter of the Great Pyramid - the exact number of days in 100 years.*
- *The measurement of a straight line of the base of the pyramid corner to corner converted to the Mean Tropical Year in days is exactly correct at 365.242.*
- *The length and the sides of the triangle converted are 365.256 days – the exact length of the Earth's solar revolution in days.*
- *The length of the sides of the pyramid converts to the exact orbital revolutions of the Earth in days at 365.259.*
- *Half the length of the diagonal of the base x 10^6 reveals the distance of the Earth from the sun.*
- *The average height of the Earth's landmass above sea level is the exact height of the Great Pyramid.*
- *Although there is a difference of opinion, it is considered by some that the Great Pyramid was built during the*

> *Age of Leo (10,500 BC) when it was aligned with the then pole star Eltanin in the constellation Draco, and at that time also with the three stars in Orion's Belt. With the shifting of the Earth it is now at the beginning of the Age of Aquarius, aligned with the pole star Polaris in the constellation of Ursa Minor and once again with the three stars in Orion's Belt.*

The actual positioning and alignment of the stones with the stars to the degree of accuracy necessary to construct it would have been impossible without lasers and infrared telescopes, which clearly indicates that the builders of the fourth dynasty Egypt did not have the engineering capacity to erect the Great Pyramid (we do not have the capacity even today!) and that this structure was used for a purpose altogether different from mere burial.'

Copyright by Nina Aldin Thune

The Nazca Lines in Peru

The Nazca Lines are gigantic geoglyphs located in the Nazca Desert, a high arid plateau which stretches fifty-three miles between the towns of Nazca and Palpa on the Pamas de Jumana in Peru. We are told they were created by the Nazca culture between 200 BC and 600 AD; but in my mind, I saw the date was 600 BC and I saw strange aircraft creating hundreds of animal patterns with a laser-type attachment, by blasting out the top layer of gravel and revealing the lighter-coloured earth underneath. The lines were first noticed in the 1920s when airplanes began flying over the Peruvian Desert.

Stonehenge

As soon as I started reading about Stonehenge the page went completely blank and I saw several aircraft with laser attachments blasting out a circle of holes. Once the holes had been excavated, which seemed to be in a matter of minutes, (perhaps because the picture was fast-forwarded), other crafts quickly flew in carrying several huge stones of varying weight and lengths. They were placed into the holes, and the aircrafts with the lasers quickly filled in the soil around the stones, and then using short blasts with the lasers, stamped the soil down around each stone. The second group then flew in carrying the huge lintel stones and placed them gently down on top of the standing stones. The picture disappeared and I was able to continue reading.

But this is very different to documented research into the construction of Stonehenge, and you may wish to read more of the latest research according to archaeological and scientific scholars. If so, go to www.stonehenge-avebury.net. My interest is also where the stones came from, and the following is quoted from the above website:
'*Not until about 2550 BC did construction of the ring of stones commence. There being no natural stone on this part of the chalk plain, the stones had to be imported.*

The first choice of stones, called bluestones, came from South West Wales, 200 km to the west. Between 60 and 80 bluestones arrived, each weighing 3-4 tons, and there was one exceptional stone at 8 tons which was placed near the centre, on the summer solstice axis, at the focus of the monument.

The later sarsen stones, weighing between 6 and 60 tons each, were dragged about 32 km (20 miles) southwards from near Avebury. Sarsens are the fractured remnants of ancient sandstone beds dating from the Eocene some 26 million years ago. The bluestones came about 2550 BC, possibly at a rate of just a few (3 to 6 say) annually. At some point delivery of the bluestones stopped. This happened before the ring of bluestones had been completed. Fairly soon afterwards, sarsen stones started arriving and their delivery is presumed to have taken one or two centuries commencing about 2500 BC.

The bluestones were rafted from Wales by sea and river. The sarsens were dragged from the Avebury Hills by haulage teams, probably aided by oxen. The stones were tipped end-first into pits dug into the sub-surface chalk. The lintels for the trilithons were raised on wooden cribs or by using earthen ramps.'

This, as I mentioned before, is very different to how I saw the construction of Stonehenge. It is my hope that more information will be revealed on this matter.

(Source: reconstruction drawing by Alan Sorrell by permission of Historic England Archives)

Petra

The ancient city of Petra, (meaning 'rock' in Greek) was literally carved from the sandstone cliffs of southern Jordan. The Petra Basin is watered by the Spring of Moses, (Ain Mousa), from which the nearby modern town of Wadi Mousa gets its name. It is here that the prophet Moses ('Musa' in Arabic), is thought to have struck a rock with his staff to extract water (Numbers 20: 10-13). The prophet Aaron, brother of Moses, died nearby and is buried atop Mount Hor (Mount Aaron) known today as Jabal Haroun.

During the Iron Age, approximately 1200 BC, the area was inhabited by the Edomites, who controlled the trade routes between the Arabian Peninsula and Damascus in what is today Syria. By the fourth century BC, the Nabataean tribe from the Arabian Peninsula moved in, and by the second century BC were firmly settled in the area with Petra as their capital. They built a civilization that stood at the crossroads of the ancient Near East, a centre for commerce as the spice routes and trading trails of the time all passed through the city. They built temples and tombs, houses and halls, altars and aqueducts. At its peak, the city of Petra was home to some 20,000 Nabataeans who, in the midst of the desert, built an ingenious system of waterways to provide their city with water.

Mysteriously the city got 'lost' for nearly 2000 years, until it was 'rediscovered' in 1812 by Swiss geographer Johannes L. Bruckhardt. Clues are still being unearthed, and today we are beginning to see what Petra once looked like 2000 years ago.

Many influences are apparent in the architecture of Petra: Assyrian, Egyptian, Hellenistic and Roman. Most of the visible remains date from the Roman period, yet bear a unique Nabataean stamp.

The only vision I saw of Petra was the front of the treasury being constructed. A picture of the front of the building was projected or printed on the front of a bare stonewall. A person in a smaller version of the craft used in the construction of Stonehenge, with a laser-type attachment, carefully proceeded to carve out the image in what seemed to be minutes. Strangely, I saw no dust or bits of rock flying off the columns as they were being carved. I was not shown any of the other buildings, and it was only recently I saw the extent of the whole complex on the internet.

The Treasury, Petra, Jordan – Creative Commons Zero – CCO

(Referral link to Max Pixel)

Crop Circles

I was not shown a flying saucer here. The only vision I saw was a very large field with four different patterns laid out beautifully. Three of the patterns had a large 'X' drawn across each one, but the fourth had the numbers '5 6 7' burned into the design. I later learned that the genuine formations are made according to the sacred or Euclidian geometry, using the vital numbers 5, 6 and 7.

Ghosts and Poltergeists

During the sixteenth and seventeenth centuries, the meaning and nature of ghosts and poltergeists was the subject of controversy between Catholic and Protestant theologians: the former seeing apparitions as evidence of souls in purgatory; while the latter interpreted them as tricks played by the Devil.

1. There are some souls who have had traumatic experiences, wake up after their RIP period on the second floor and just refuse to believe they have left their physical bodies behind. They turn inwards, (much like a sulky teenager!) and all they want to do is stay in bed in a semi-dream state and plot and dream revenge on those who caused their situation. These are the poltergeists and other naughty (evil) spirits, wanting to take out their frustration by tormenting whoever they feel like. They are usually attracted by fear, or by someone who is experiencing a glimmer of being psychic, such as the mediums and spiritual healers of the future.

2. There are others who cannot come to terms with what has happened to them and constantly want to

go in search for their bodies that they left behind, or someone close who had died with them on the Earth plane. They are trapped in their era and can only accept the situation when they are made to understand by a person on Earth who is able to point them in the right direction.

3. The souls of these spirits continue to stay in bed and, in their dreams, they are able to visit the Earth plane. I saw them moving in a way similar to a person on Earth having an out-of-body experience. Some psychics are able to see and/or feel them, and are able to guide them to a higher plane.

4. For some this can go on for centuries, as they remain trapped in the period of their time until they are helped on their way. The hierarchy allows this situation to carry on as a reminder, or a sort of 'teaser' to those on the Earth plane that there is another dimension somewhere else, thus prompting those brave enough to investigate this phenomenon to do so.

To Sum Up

Think of Earth as a school. It has different classrooms carrying different frequencies to support different expressions of culture. Each culture has its own language, its own music, and its own frequencies.

During hundreds of years, each soul must experience many situations and learn many lessons, and a vast proportion of those years will be spend incarnated on the Earth plane; but there will also be many lives spent behind the scenes helping the souls cross over during accidents and/or during catastrophic occurrences such as tsunamis and earthquakes etc.

The Law of Cause and Effect

Life on Earth is governed by the law of cause and effect, and stumbling blocks are set in our paths before us, in order for us to experience certain situations and learn to cope with them to the best of our ability. We hopefully learn from our mistakes; but if we don't, we will have to experience the similar situation, or situations in a future life.

When the more mature souls arrive 'home' from the Earth plane, their lives are assessed by themselves and the elders. After a break, they are allowed to choose the next path they wish to take on Earth. They can choose to work behind the scenes for a while, or go back as soon as possible to try to get their lives on the Earth plane over as soon as possible.

There is no absolute freewill, however, in relation to birth and death on Earth. Neither are there coincidences in life on Earth. You are born and die at specific times, even if you commit suicide. The lesson here is for everyone concerned to deal with the *cause* and with the *effect* it creates to the best of their ability.

Understandably, there is no freewill for a child until they are mature enough to follow their own path, and when they are, that is when humans are permitted a limited amount of choice in life. They are born into a specific nation and family, and guided by their elders according to the customs and religions of the country of their birth.

Through out your adult journey on the Earth plane, there are many milestones to reach along your path, and the freewill you do have is to choose which road to take to reach the next milestone. You can take the straight and narrow, the short cut, or the long way around through the scenic route. But no matter which route you take, however, you will always end up at the next milestone in your life. The milestones are the important places you have to reach in order to meet someone, or deal with a particular situation that has been put in your way.

An example:

On the way to catch a plane to attend an interview for a fantastic job abroad, you are delayed on the motorway, miss your flight and the plane you were supposed to be on explodes in mid-air. How will you deal with the situation? a) Try your utmost to reschedule? b) Shrug your shoulders and say, 'I can't be bothered now; I'm going to the pub to settle my nerves'? Whatever road you choose will be the right one for you.

The a) road *could* get you the job because the new employers were impressed by the way you handled the situation, *or*, not get you the job because you were not qualified enough, but this could mean you have reached the place you should be at, but not in the right job for you. The b) road takes you to the pub, where you meet your future spouse or employer, *or*, you drown your sorrows, go home, sleep it off and decide you've had enough, life sucks, and go on social benefits. This is another test. Are you going to pick yourself up and try again, or is this where you choose to be for the rest of your life?

And this is the beauty of choice, and life, and freewill; but remember that whichever path you choose, it is where you are eventually meant to be.

Also remember, as mentioned before, we are created in family groups and they are our soulmates, and your other half is your twin soul. You are separated right after you were created and do not meet again until your last lives, or on the eighth plane after many centuries if one of you completes life on the Earth plane before the other one; but it is possible that you may catch a glimpse of your twin soul during your various incarnations.

Some souls choose to have only one profession or career, and all those at the top of their profession or craft, in every walk of life, are the older souls who have learned their skills throughout many lives. It is not possible to be at the top in this computerised, scientific and technological world we live in today without the experience gained in previous lives. And part of the process of arriving here is to test our relationships and how we accept the criticism of peers and family, learning self-control along the way.

For example, a couple who are young souls might have a very talented child who can read or do advanced maths, or is able to play the violin or piano by the age of three or four. (Some couples will find it very difficult to cope with having a child more advanced that they are.) These children are old souls who have chosen these particular situations for karmic reasons. But it is how the parents of this talented child respond to it that teaches them about themselves, and helps them to progress through their own learning.

Remember, too, that every one of us has our own spiritual name. This is your true name and will depict the first era or century you were born into. You will have many names during your lives on Earth, but you will only have one unique spiritual name belonging only to you. Helpers such as guides sometimes have names of Red Indians and/or Tibetan monks; an angel could be someone from the time of the Old Testament, in which case they will have a biblical name. Or you may have a name from the Egyptian, Greek or Roman eras, if your soul was created during those times. As mentioned before, it is possible that your spiritual name could be revealed to you once you fully understand your role during a particular time in your life plan. The new souls being born in this era could very well be a Gavin or a Stacey!

Looking out for Signs to Help you Along the way

I mentioned before that there are no coincidences in life. Once you realise that everything is as it should be, you become aware of little signs intended to comfort you or make you aware that you are exactly in the place you are supposed to be. Some can be really trivial or silly, whereas others will fill you with love and understanding. Below are a few examples:

1. A loved one has recently died. You walk along the street, and there is a delivery van parked with the name of your beloved included in the firm's logo. A little reminder you were intended to walk down that particular street at that specific time.

2. You are feeling sad, you open an old handbag and find a little trinket you'd received from your departed loved one, which you thought you had lost a long time ago. It doesn't mean that they had specifically arranged all this, as perhaps you simply forgot to look for the trinket in that place.

3. Or you had been thinking of your dear departed Mum
    before walking into a shop and there her favourite
    tune was playing softly in the background. It might
    seem like a trivial coincidence, and nothing to do with
    your Mum arranging this from the "other side", but a
    subtle little sign to show you that you were in the right
    place at the right time, for what ever reason.

4. You miss your bus, take the next one, and there is a
    neighbour on the bus whom you haven't seen for a
    long time. This could be good or bad, but rest assured,
    there will be some unfinished business to be dealt with.
    Good: you are very happy because you had lost touch.
    Your daughters were once very good friends, and you
    have been trying to contact her to invite them to the
    wedding. Bad: before you moved a few years ago, you
    had borrowed their lawn mower, and it just happened,
    in error (?), to move with you and unfortunately for
    the neighbour you forgot (?) to leave a forwarding
    address. She waves and beckons to you to come and sit
    next to her. How do you handle this situation?

There are many other little signs to look out for, for instance:

5. You could be thinking of someone, perhaps an old
    flame, and you walk into a shop and, guess what? You
    bump into each other.

6. You could be thinking of someone for a while when
    the phone rings, and that very person is on the line.

7. You walk past a shop and there is the dress you have
    been searching for for ages in the window. You rush in,
    it's your size, and you buy it. This was no coincidence,
    you were meant to see that dress.

8. You are thinking of a particular place or subject, you turn on the TV or radio and there is a discussion regarding this very subject you had been thinking about. This particular situation often happens to me. Especially when I'm feeling a little low.

I've had many signs throughout these past years. Some made me smile, but most of them were comforting. The following one lasted on and off for years.

My husband and I had been to the Lakes for a break, and on the way home he said I should have a go at driving on the motorway. I was not very happy. I have been driving for many years, but the motorways here in the UK are rather scary! As I got onto the road, there was a blue delivery van with a white arrow logo painted on the side. After a while my husband said, 'That person in the blue van is a very good driver; watch him as he moves carefully in and out of the lanes, and follow his example.' This went on for many miles when it suddenly struck me that a few weeks previously I had read a book about a woman who had past life regression and had gone back to a life as a Red Indian . . . and her husband's name was White Arrow.

This white arrow became a comforting sign for many years. For example, I would be driving or walking from town feeling miserable and downhearted and the van would drive past. And there was one very, very bad day when I was feeling so desperately unhappy. I was lying on the sofa thinking to my self *if only I had the courage I would end my life* when there was a knock on the door. It was a parcel for my neighbour, who happened to be out, and there at the bottom of our drive the white arrow delivery van was parked.

That little sign once again gave me the courage to be able to face another day.

Final Thoughts

I do sincerely hope this book will help to explain why sad and distressing things happen to you. When you sometimes think *why me? why us? why did my little baby die?*

It will not ease your pain completely, but it might help you to understand the reason why things happen that we find hard.

I am just a messenger from another dimension who has been instructed to share these visions and thoughts with you, and I hope that my writing this has been helpful to you.

June Rye
January 2012

oooOooo